G. SCHIRMER'S
COLLECTION OF
OPERA LIBRETTOS

RIGOLETTO

Opera in Four Acts

Music by

Giuseppe Verdi

Libretto by
FRANCESCO MARIA PIAVE
After Victor Hugo's play *Le Roi s'amuse*

English Version by
RUTH and THOMAS MARTIN

Ed. 2530

G. SCHIRMER *New York / London*

RIGOLETTO

Verdi (1813-1901) composed *Rigoletto* in 1851, when he was thirty-seven years old. His sixteenth opera, it started a new phase in his career. Until then he had written mostly heroic music that had inspired the Italian patriots and made him a national figure; now he began to translate human emotions into passionate or tender melodies that made him a world celebrity. *Rigoletto* is the earliest Verdi work in the standard repertory; *La Traviata* and *Il Trovatore* came two years later, *Aida* two decades. When he wrote *Rigoletto,* Verdi said that he wanted to give his music "character"; an example is the famous Quartet in the fourth act, in which each of the four voices singing together expresses a different feeling.

In 1850, when the Teatro la Fenice in Venice asked Verdi for a new opera, he decided to adapt a melodrama by the French playwright Victor Hugo; it was called *Le Roi s'amuse,* and the frivolous king, almost victimized by his hunchbacked jester, was supposed to be François I of France. The play had been given in Paris in 1832, provoking a scandal. Verdi's imagination was stirred by its human problems, which Francesco Maria Piave translated into an effective libretto. The composer was progressing well with the music when the censor objected to the theme on moral grounds; the real reason, however, was that Venice still chafed under Austrian control, and the police feared that a plot showing a monarch in an unfavorable light might provoke demonstrations. Verdi ultimately agreed to change the locale and the names of the characters; the King of France became an imaginary "Duke of Mantua" — now a household name.

Venice cheered the new and exciting opera at its premiere on March 11, 1851, and especially the Duke's cavatina, "La donna è mobile." Verdi, realizing how singable it was, had not shown it even to the tenor until two days before the performance, so that it would not be sung by the gondoliers before it was sung in the theater. It has since remained among the most popular operatic arias. In America, the opera was first given at the Academy of Music in New York on February 9, 1855.

A.M.L.

Courtesy of Opera News

THE STORY

ACT I. Strolling among the courtiers who throng the ballroom of his palace, the Duke of Mantua boasts of his many amorous conquests. His hunchbacked jester, Rigoletto, suggests that his master win the beautiful Countess Ceprano by imprisoning her husband. Ceprano, furious, vows in revenge to abduct a young girl whom he believes to be Rigoletto's mistress. When Monterone, an elderly noble, forces his way in to denounce the Duke for seducing his daughter, he is mocked by Rigoletto, sure of his master's protection. As Monterone is led away to prison by the guards, he curses the jester, who falls to the floor in horror.

ACT II. Brooding over the curse, Rigoletto hurries late at night to the house where he has hidden his beloved daughter, Gilda. Before he reaches his gate he is accosted by Sparafucile, a professional assassin, who offers his services for a fee. But Rigoletto dismisses him, reflecting bitterly that his tongue works as much harm as the assassin's dagger. The mood of the jester softens when he is greeted by Gilda; lonesome in her seclusion, the girl embraces her father and begs him to tell her the story of her mother, who died long ago. Rigoletto sadly replies that his wife was an angel, adding that now Gilda is all he has left to love in the world. Ever fearful for his daughter's safety, he summons her nurse, Giovanna, whom he warns not to admit anyone to the house. As the jester leaves, the Duke himself slips past him into the garden. Pitching a purse of coins to Giovanna as a bribe, he declares his love for the astonished Gilda, telling her that he is a poor student named Gaultier Maldè. When footsteps are heard in the street, Gilda pleads with him to flee. Alone, she dwells tenderly on his name before ascending the staircase to her room. Meanwhile, the malicious courtiers, incited by Ceprano, stop Rigoletto in the dark street and ask his aid in abducting Ceprano's wife, who lives across the way. Relieved, the jester allows himself to be masked like the others, but the courtiers blindfold him instead. In his confusion Rigoletto places their ladder against his own wall, while the courtiers laugh among themselves at their chance to outwit him; they break into his house and quickly carry off Gilda. At the sound of the girl's muffled cry for help, the duped jester tears the blindfold from his eyes to find himself alone. Seized with terror, he rushes into the garden, discovers Gilda's scarf and, after searching her room, reappears in anguish.

ACT III. The Duke paces a room in his palace, fearing that his courtiers have robbed him of Gilda, whom he imagines in lonely tears. When the courtiers return to tell him they have brought the girl to his chamber, the libertine rushes to the conquest. Soon Rigoletto enters searching for Gilda, who, he confesses to the indifferent courtiers, is his daughter. Though astonished, they bar his way to the Duke's quarters, at which the jester lashes out at them for their cruelty and treachery, ending his tirade with a plea for mercy. At that very moment Gilda appears, disheveled in her nightdress; she runs in shame to her father, who orders the courtiers to leave. When they are alone, the girl tells her father of the long courtship of the Duke, whom she had seen each week at Mass. As Monterone is led through the corridors, the enraged Rigoletto swears to avenge his wrongs; Gilda, out of love, begs for the Duke's pardon.

ACT IV. on a dark night, Rigoletto and Gilda lurk outside the lonely inn to which Sparafucile, aided by his voluptuous sister, Maddalena, lures his victims. The jester forces Gilda to watch the Duke, disguised as a soldier, make love to Maddalena, laughing all the while at the fickleness of woman; while Maddalena leads her intended victim on, the jester comforts his daughter in the shadows outside. He tells the girl to go home, dress herself as a boy and then meet him in Verona; he pays Sparafucile to murder the Duke and departs. As a storm brews, Gilda returns to overhear Maddalena urge her brother to spare the handsome stranger and kill Rigoletto instead. Shocked by her lack of professional ethics, Sparafucile refuses, but at length he agrees to substitute the next guest who comes to the inn. Gilda, glad to sacrifice herself to save the Duke, knocks on the door at the height of the storm, is pulled into the inn and fatally stabbed. Before long, Rigoletto returns to collect the body of the Duke. The jester gloats over the sack the assassin gives him to dump in the nearby river, but on hearing the supposedly dead libertine's voice in the distance, he frantically cuts open the sack to find his daughter's crumpled body. Asking forgiveness, Gilda tells Rigoletto that she goes to join her mother in heaven. When she dies, the distraught father cries that Monterone's curse has been fulfilled.

Courtesy of Opera News

CAST OF CHARACTERS

THE DUKE OF MANTUA . . . . Tenor

BORSA, a courtier . . . . Tenor

THE COUNTESS CEPRANO . . . . Mezzo-soprano

RIGOLETTO, the Duke's jester, a hunchback . . . . Baritone

COUNT CEPRANO, a nobleman . . . . Bass

MARULLO, a courtier . . . . Baritone

COUNT MONTERONE, a nobleman . . . . Baritone

SPARAFUCILE, a professional assassin . . . . Bass

GILDA, daughter of Rigoletto . . . . Soprano

GIOVANNA, Gilda's nurse . . . . Mezzo-soprano

A PAGE . . . . Soprano

A HERALD . . . . Baritone

MADDALENA, sister of Sparafucile . . . . Contralto

Courtiers, Ladies and Gentlemen of the Court, Servants.

PLACE: Mantua, Italy

TIME: Sixteenth century

SYNOPSIS OF SCENES

RIGOLETTO

ATTO I

Sala magnifica nel Palazzo Ducale
(Il Duca e Borsa che vengono da una
porta del fondo.)

DUCA

Della mia bella incognita borghese
Toccare il fin dell' avventura io voglio.

BORSA

Di quella giovin che vedete al tempio?

DUCA

Da tre mesi ogni festa.

BORSA

La sua dimora?

DUCA

In un remoto calle;
Misterioso un uom v'entra ogni notte.

BORSA

E sa colei chi sia l' amante suo?

DUCA

Lo ignora.

(Un gruppo di dame e cavalieri attra-
versano la sala.)

BORSA

Quante beltà! Mirate.

DUCA

Le vince tutte di Cepran la sposa.

BORSA

Non v'oda il Conte, o Duca!

DUCA

A me che importa?

BORSA

Dirlo ad altra ei potria.

DUCA

Nè sventura per me certo saria . . .

Questa o quella per me pari sono
A quant'altre d'intorno mi vedo;
Del mio core l'impero non cedo
Meglio ad una che ad altra beltà.
La costoro avvenenza è qual dono
Di che il fato ne infiora la vita;
S'oggi questa mi torna gradita
Forse un'altra doman lo sarà.
La costanza, tiranna del core,
Detestiamo qual morbo crudele.
Sol chi vuole si serbi fedele;
Non v'ha amor se non v'è libertà.
De' mariti il geloso furore,
Degli amanti le smanie derido;
Anco d'Argo i cent' occhi disfido
Se mi punge una qualche beltà.

(Il Conte di Ceprano, che segue da
lungi la sua sposa seguita da un'altro
Cavaliere. Dame e signori entrano da
varie parti.)

DUCA

(Alla Signora di Ceprano, movendo ad
incontrarla con molta galanteria.)

Partite? Crudele!

LA CONTESSA

Seguire lo sposo m' è forza a Ceprano.

DUCA

Ma dee luminoso
In corte tal astro qual sole brillar.
Per voi qui ciascuno dovrà palpitar.
Per voi già possente la fiamma d' amore
Inebria, conquide, distrugge il mio core.

LA CONTESSA

Calmatevi.

(Le dà il braccio ed esce con lei.)

RIGOLETTO *(al Conte Cepriano.)*

In testa che avete,
Signor di Ceprano?

(Ceprano fa un gesto d' impazienza e
segue il Duca.)

RIGOLETTO *(ai Cortigiani.)*

Ei sbuffa, vedete?

RIGOLETTO

ACT I

A magnificent hall in the ducal palace.

DUKE

(*enters from another hall, conversing with Borsa*)

This very night I will finish my adventure
With that young girl I followed through the city!

BORSA

Is this the girl you noticed Sunday morning?

DUKE

Ev'ry Sunday for three months now.

BORSA

Where will you find her?

DUKE

She lives not far from here.
Ev'ry night a stranger comes to see her.

BORSA

And does she know the name of her admirer?

DUKE

Of course not!
(*A group of ladies and cavaliers crosses the stage.*)

BORSA

Beauties galore! Enchanting!

DUKE

But none can equal the Countess of Ceprano!

BORSA

Don't let her husband hear that!

DUKE

And why should I care?

BORSA

He is jealous and spiteful.

DUKE

Then this conquest would be twice as delightful!

Charming women,
Whatever their name and rank,
I always pursue them with equal abandon.
At my pleasure I wander at random
To find adventure wherever I turn.
I delight in the thrill of their beauty;
Only they make my life exciting.
If today one should beckon inviting,
Then tomorrow for another my passion may burn!

To be faithful is not my intention,
I detest this unwelcome, tyrannic convention.
To such slavery I'll never surrender,
For love is poor indeed if your freedom is lost.
Jealous husbands and ill-tempered lovers
Only move me to scorn and derision.
I defy them with undaunted decision;
I must conquer wife and sweetheart,
Never minding the cost.
(*The minuet is danced. The Duke addresses the Countess Ceprano.*)

DUKE

You're leaving? Dear Countess!

COUNTESS

My duty commands me to stay with Ceprano.

DUKE

Your beauty is so radiant,
Surpassing all others, alluring and glorious!
You reign like a goddess in splendor victorious.
My own heart is flaming, desiring, imploring;
Behold me, tormented, admiring, adoring!

COUNTESS

You flatter me.

DUKE

(*gives his arm to the Countess and leaves with her*)

RIGOLETTO

(*who has observed the scene, calls after him, mockingly*)

Great Honor has come
to the house of Ceprano!
(*Count Ceprano makes a gesture of annoyance and follows them.*)
(*to the Courtiers*)

He's fuming! You saw it!

CORO

Che festa!
Il duca quì pur si diverte.

RIGOLETTO

Così non è sempre? Che nuove scoperte.
Il giuoco ed il vino, le feste, la danza
Battaglie, conviti, ben tutto gli sta.
Or della Contessa l' assedio egli avanza.
E intanto il marito fremendo ne va.

(*Esce.*)

(*Marullo entra premuroso.*)

MARULLO

Gran nuova! Gran nuova!

CORO

Che avvenne? parlate!

MARULLO

Stupir ne dovrete!

CORO

Narrate, narrate!

MARULLO

Ah! ah! Rigoletto . . .

CORO

Ebben?

MARULLO

Caso enorme!

CORO

Perduto ha la gobba? non è più difforme?

MARULLO

Più strana è la cosa! il pazzo
possiede . . .

CORO

Infine?

MARULLO

Un' amante!

CORO

Un' amante! Chi il crede?

MARULLO

Il gobbo in Cupido or s'è trasformato!

CORO

Quel mostro Cupido! Cupido beato!

(*Il Duca rientra seguito da Rigoletto,
indi Ceprano.*)

DUCA

Ah, più di Ceprano importuno non v' è!
La cara sua sposa è un angiol per me.

RIGOLETTO

Rapitela.

DUCA

È detto! ma il farlo?

RIGOLETTO

Stasera.

DUCA

Non pensi tu al Conte?

RIGOLETTO

Non c'è la prigione?

DUCA

Ah, no.

RIGOLETTO

Ebben . . . s'esilia.

DUCA

Nemmeno, buffone.

RIGOLETTO

Allora la testa?

(*Indicando di farla tagliare.*)

CEPRANO (*da se.*)

(Oh l'anima nera!)

DUCA

Che di', questa testa?

RIGOLETTO

È ben naturale.
Che far di tal testa? A cosa ella vale?

CEPRANO

(*Infuriato battendo la spada.*)
Marrano!

DUCA (*a Ceprano.*)
Fermate!

RIGOLETTO

Da rider mi fa.

CORO

In furia è montato!

DUCA

Buffone, vien quà.
Ah sempre tu spingi lo scherzo all'
estremo,
Quell' ira che sfidi colpirti potrà.

COURTIERS
Delightful!
The Duke is pursuing his pleasure.

RIGOLETTO
Is that so unusual?
When has he been diff'rent?
Our Duke is enjoying himself to the fullest,
Carousing in mirth on his lighthearted path.
And now he is wooing the Countess Ceprano,
And meanwhile her husband is seething with wrath!

(he leaves)

MARULLO (enters excitedly)
Sensation! Sensation!

COURTIERS
What happened? Let's hear it!

MARULLO
I want you to guess it!

COURTIERS
How can we? You tell us!

MARULLO
Ha, ha! Rigoletto!

COURTIERS
Well, what?

MARULLO
It's too fantastic!

COURTIERS
The ugly old braggart?
Has somebody tricked him?

MARULLO
It's even more drastic!
The fool now is keeping . . .

COURTIERS
Continue!

MARULLO
A mistress!

COURTIERS
A mistress! It can't be!

MARULLO
The hunchback is playing the role of a Romeo!

COURTIERS
The hunchback? A Romeo?
I cannot believe it!

DUKE
(re-enters, followed by Rigoletto)
The Count of Ceprano's becoming a bore!
His wife is an angel I madly adore.

RIGOLETTO
Make love to her!

DUKE
With pleasure, but when?

RIGOLETTO
This evening.

DUKE
And what of Ceprano?

RIGOLETTO
We'll put him in prison!

DUKE
We can't.

RIGOLETTO
Well then . . . we'll ban him.

DUKE
We can't do that either.

RIGOLETTO
In that case . . . why don't we behead him?

CEPRANO (aside)
You meanest of scoundrels!

DUKE (patting Ceprano's shoulder)
Remember, I like him.

RIGOLETTO
Why can't we behead him?
One head is a trifle!
There are plenty of others!

CEPRANO
(furiously, brandishing his sword)
You villain!

DUKE (to Ceprano)
He's joking!

RIGOLETTO
Ridiculous dunce!

COURTIERS
Ceprano is furious!

DUKE
Now stop it at once!
(to Rigoletto)
You'd better be careful or else you'll be sorry!

RIGOLETTO

Che coglier mi puote? Di loro non temo;
Del duca il protetto nessun toccherà.

CEPRANO

(*Ai Cortigiani, a parte.*)
Vendetta dal pazzo!

CORO

Contr' esso un rancore
Pei tristi suoi modi, di noi chi non ha?

CEPRANO

Vendetta!

CORO

Ma come?

CEPRANO

In armi chi ha core doman sia da me,
A notte.

TUTTI

Sì. Sarà.

CEPRANO, CORTIGIANI

Vendetta del pazzo!
Contr'esso un rancore
Pei tristi suoi modi di noi chi non ha?

TUTTI

Tutto è gioia, tutto è festa!
Tutto invitaci a goder!
Oh, guardate, non par questa
Or la reggia del piacer!

MONTERONE (*Dall' interno.*)
Ch' io gli parli.

DUCA

No.

MONTERONE (*entrando.*)
Il voglio.

TUTTI

Monterone!

MONTERONE

Si, Monteron! La voce mia qual tuono
Vi scuoterà dovunque!

RIGOLETTO

(*al Duca, contraffacendo la voce di Monterone.*)
Ch' io gli parli.

(*Si avanza con ridicola gravità.*)

Voi congiuraste contro noi, signore,
E noi, clementi in vero, perdonammo.

Qual vi piglia or delirio a tutte l'ore
Di vostra figlia a reclamar l' onore?

MONTERONE

Novello insulto! Ah sì, a turbare,
Sarò vostr'orgie, verrò a gridare,
Fino a che vegga restarsi inulto
Di mia famiglia l'atroce insulto;
E se al carnefice pur mi darete,
Spettro terribile mi rivedrete,
Portante in mano il teschio mio,
Vendetta chiedere al mondo, a Dio.

DUCA

Non più, arrestatelo.

RIGOLETTO

È matto!

CORO

Quai detti!

MONTERONE

Ah, siate entrambi, voi maledetti.
Slanciare il cane al leon morente
È vile, o Duca—e tu serpente,

(*a Rigoletto.*)

Tu che d' un padre ridi al dolore
Sii maledetto!

RIGOLETTO (*Da sè colpito.*)

Che sento? Orrore!

TUTTI (*meno Rigoletto.*)

Oh tu che la festa audace hai turbato,
Da un genio d' inferno qui fosti guidato;
È vano ogni detto, di quà t' allontana,
Va, trema, vegliardo, dell' ira sovrana.
Tu l' hai provocata, più speme non v' è,
Un' ora fatale fu questa per te.

RIGOLETTO

What harm could befall me? I've no
   need to worry!
The Duke's gracious favor makes up
   for them all.
CEPRANO (*to the other Courtiers*)
I call you to vengeance!

COURTIERS

There's no one among us who bears
   him no grudge!

CEPRANO

Agreed then?

COURTIERS

Yes, agreed.
The fool must be punished,
Revenge is in order,
His sharp, evil tongue has offended
   us all.
We'll take revenge!
Yes, rely on us all.
On to vengeance!

RIGOLETTO, DUKE

Let's have music!
Let's have dancing!

ALL

Let's have music,
Let's have dancing,
Nothing shall disturb our pleasure,
Let's enjoy in fullest measure
Charming women, wine and play!

MONTERONE (*off-stage*)

I want to talk to him,

DUKE

No!

MONTERONE

It must be. (*he appears*)

COURTIERS

Monterone!

MONTERONE

Yes, it is I,
My voice like warning thunder
Shall ev'rywhere pursue you!

RIGOLETTO (*imitating Monterone*)

I want to talk to him.

(*mockingly*)

You have conspired brazenly
   against us;
However, we have bestowed on you
   our gracious pardon.
Yet you stand here before us

And choose to bore us
With endless speeches
About your daughter's honor.

MONTERONE

A new injustice.
Another insult and defamation
You heaped upon me, my name and
   station.
But I shall clamor for retribution
For my own daughter's offended honor
And if you sentence me to execution
I shall continue my persecution.
As ghastly vision I'll come to haunt you.
And cry anathema before the world,
Before the world and God Almighty!

DUKE

Enough, arrest him!

RIGOLETTO

He's raving!

BORSA, MARULLO, CEPRANO

How dare he!

MONTERONE

May both of you forever be cursed!
To hurl your dogs against the dying
   lion,
Oh Duke, is shameful;

(*to Rigoletto*)

And you, his henchman,
You who deride the grief of a father,
My curse upon you!

RIGOLETTO

(*terror-stricken, to himself*)

Oh heaven, he cursed me!

DUKE, COURTIERS

You foolish intruder and spreader of
   terror,
This time you've committed your last
   fatal error.
Away with your curses and vile accusa-
   tion,
Beware of the Duke and his just in-
   dignation.
For you there is nothing but sorrow in
   store,
In prison's seclusion you'll try him no
   more!
(*Monterone is led away by two guards.
   All others follow the Duke into another room.*)

ATTO II

*L'estremità più deserta d' una via cieca,
Casa di Rigoletto a terrazzo.*

(*Rigoletto chiuso nel suo mantello. Sparafucile lo segue portando sotto il mantello una lunga spada.*)

RIGOLETTO

(Quel vecchio maledivami!)

SPARAFUCILE

Signor?

RIGOLETTO

Va, non ho niente.

SPARAFUCILE

Nè il chiesi . . . a voi presente
Un uom di spada sta.

RIGOLETTO

Un ladro?

SPARAFUCILE

Un uom che libera per poco da un
    rivale,
E voi ne avete . . .

RIGOLETTO

Quale?

SPARAFUCILE

La vostra donna è là.

RIGOLETTO

(Che sento!) E quanto spendere
Per un signor dovrei?

SPARAFUCILE

Prezzo maggior vorrei.

RIGOLETTO

Com'usasi pagar?

SPARAFUCILE

Una metà s'anticipa,
Il resto si dà poi.

RIGOLETTO

(Demonio!) E come puoi
Tanto securo oprar?

SPARAFUCILE

Soglio in cittade uccidere,
Oppure nel mio tetto.
L'uomo di sera aspetto;
Una stoccata . . . e muor.

RIGOLETTO

(Demonio!) E come in casa?

SPARAFUCILE

È facile:
M'aiuta mia sorella.
Per le vie danza, è bella.
Chi voglio attira . . . e allor . . .

RIGOLETTO

Comprendo.

SPARAFUCILE

Senza strepito . . .

RIGOLETTO

Comprendo . . .

SPARAFUCILE

È questo il mio strumento.
                    (*Mostra la spada.*)
Vi serve?

RIGOLETTO

No . . . al momento.

SPARAFUCILE

Peggio per voi . . .

RIGOLETTO

Chi sa?

SPARAFUCILE

Sparafucil mi nomino.

RIGOLETTO

Straniero?

SPARAFUCILE (*Per andarsene.*)
Borgognone.

RIGOLETTO

E dove all' occasione?

SPARAFUCILE

Quì sempre a sera.

RIGOLETTO

Va.   (*Sparafucile parte.*)

ACT II

*The end of a dead-end street. At left a
house of modest appearance with a
small courtyard, surrounded by a
wall. In the courtyard a large tree
and a marble seat. In the wall a door
that leads to the street. Above the
wall a terrace supported by arches.
The door on the second floor goes to
that terrace, which is reached by a
staircase from the front. At the oppo-
site side of the street is the palace of
Ceprano. It is night.*

RIGOLETTO

(appears, wrapped in his cloak)
How heavy weighs his curse on me!

SPARAFUCILE

*(who had followed him from a distance,
carrying a long sword under his
cloak)*
One word.

RIGOLETTO

Go, I've no money.

SPARAFUCILE

I ask none.
An expert swordsman presents himself
    to you.

RIGOLETTO

A bandit?

SPARAFUCILE

A man who'll rid you of a rival for a
    pittance.
You do have rivals . . .

RIGOLETTO

Have I?

SPARAFUCILE

The one you love is in there.

RIGOLETTO *(to himself, worried)*
Who told him? *(aloud)*
And for a nobleman, how much would
    you require?

SPARAFUCILE

That would be somewhat higher!

RIGOLETTO

And how would you be paid?

SPARAFUCILE

Half of the sum before the deed,
The other when it's done.

RIGOLETTO *(to himself)*
A demon! *(aloud)*
How can you safely ply such a dang'r-
    ous trade?

SPARAFUCILE

Sometimes in lonely thoroughfares,
Or better in my own house,
Waiting at night in ambush,
I stab my victims, they fall . . .

RIGOLETTO

A savage! And in your dwelling?

SPARAFUCILE

That's easier.
My sister's charm procures them,
She is wily, clever, seductive!
She slyly lures them, that's all . . .

RIGOLETTO

I follow . . .

SPARAFUCILE

Very quietly . . .

RIGOLETTO

I follow . . .

SPARAFUCILE

(drawing out his dagger)
This dagger fells the traitor.
Agreed, then?

RIGOLETTO

No, maybe later . . .

SPARAFUCILE

(hiding the dagger again)
Very unwise . . .

RIGOLETTO

Who knows?

SPARAFUCILE

Sparafucile awaits your call . . .

RIGOLETTO

You're foreign?

SPARAFUCILE

A Burgundian.

RIGOLETTO

Supposing I want to find you?

SPARAFUCILE

Here any evening.

Go!   RIGOLETTO

*(Sparafucile disappears in the dark
    night.)*

RIGOLETTO

(*guardando dietro a Sparafucile.*)

Pari siamo! Io la lingua, egli ha il
    pugnale;
L'uomo son io che ride, ei quel che
    spegne!
Quel vecchio maledivami . . .
O uomini! O natura!
Vil scellerato mi faceste voi!
O rabbia! Esser difforme!
O rabbia! Esser buffone . . .
Non dover, non poter altro che ridere!
Il retaggio d'ogni uom m'è tolto; il
    pianto.
Questo padrone mio,
Giovin, giocondo, sì possente, bello,
Sonnecchiando mi dice:
Fa ch'io rida, buffone!
Forzarmi deggio a farlo! Oh danna-
    zione!
Odio a voi, cortigiani schernitori!
Quanta in mordervi ho gioia!
Se iniquo son, per cagion vostra è solo.
Ma in altr'uomo qui mi cangio! . . .
Quel vecchio maledivami! Tal pensiero
Perchè conturba ognor la mente mia?
Mi coglierà sventura? . . . Ah no, è
    follia!

(*Apre con chiave, ed entra nel cortile.
Gilda esce dalla casa e si getta nelle
sue braccia.*)

RIGOLETTO

Figlia!

GILDA

Mio padre!

RIGOLETTO

A te d'appresso.
Trova sol gioia il core oppresso.

GILDA

Oh quanto amore!

RIGOLETTO

Mia vita sei!
Senza te in terra qual bene avrei?

(*Sospira.*)

GILDA

Voi sospirate! Che v'ange tanto?
Lo dite a questa povera figlia.

Se v'ha mistero, per lei sia franto,
Ch'ella conosca la sua famiglia . . .

RIGOLETTO

Tu non ne hai . . .

GILDA

Qual nome avete?

RIGOLETTO

A te che importa?

GILDA

Se non volete
Di voi parlarmi . . .

RIGOLETTO (*Interrompendola.*)
Non uscir mai.

GILDA

Non vo che al tempio.

RIGOLETTO

Oh, ben tu fai.

GILDA

Se non di voi, almen chi sia
Fate ch' io sappia la madre mia.

RIGOLETTO

Ah! Deh, non parlare al misero
Del suo perduto bene.
Ella sentia, quell'angelo,
Pietà delle mie pene.
Solo, difforme, povero,
Per compassion mi amò.
Ah! Morìa, morìa . . . le zolle coprano
Lievi quel capo amato.
Sola or tu resti al misero,
O Dio, sii ringraziato!

GILDA

Oh! Quanto dolor! Che spremere
Sì amaro pianto può?
Padre, non più, calmatevi,
Mi lacera tal vista.
Il nome vostro ditemi,
Il duol che si v' attrista.

RIGOLETTO

A che nomarmi? È inutile!
Padre ti sono, e basti.
Me forse al mondo temono,
D' alcuno ho forse gli asti.
Altri mi maledicono.

RIGOLETTO

(*alone, looking after Sparafucile*)

We are equal!
I, the jester, and he the murd'rer!
I stab with cold derision,
He with the dagger.
How heavy weighs that curse on me!
Oh mankind, oh creation!
You are the reason I am vile and
    vicious!
Oh torture, being a cripple!
Oh torture, wearing a foolscap!
Night and day I must laugh,
Shamming hilarity!
I'm denied man's relief in sorrow,
Consoling tears!
There is my noble master,
Youthful and carefree,
Always happy, handsome,
Who cammands when he pleases:
"Come, my fool, and amuse me!"
And I must always do so!
Loathsome profession!
I destest you, you debased and scornful
    courtiers!
How I gloat when I can hurt you!
If I am a villain,
Only to you I owe it!
But in my home I am another!
How heavy weighs that curse on me!
It pursues me, it preys upon my mind!
Why do I hear it?
Could it forebode misfortune?
Ah no, I don't fear it!

(*He enters his courtyard. Gilda comes
    from the house and throws herself into
    his arms.*)

Gilda!

GILDA

My father!

RIGOLETTO

When you're beside me,
You bring a joy too often denied me!

GILDA

Always and always!

RIGOLETTO

I love you dearly!
You bring me sunshine when you are
    near me!

(*he sighs*)

GILDA

But you are troubled!
I cannot bear it!
Oh tell me, I beg you,

Please, Father, tell me!
If there's a secret clouding your spirit,
Who but your daughter rather should
    share it?

RIGOLETTO

I will not say!

GILDA

Tell me, who are you?

RIGOLETTO

What does it matter?

GILDA

If then your own life must be a secret . . .

RIGOLETTO (*interrupting her*)

Have you been out?

GILDA

To church on Sunday . . .

RIGOLETTO

Then all is well.

GILDA

You guard this secret
Yet there's another;
Will you not tell me about my mother?

RIGOLETTO

Ah! Do not recall those memories,
Mem'ries of vanished happiness . . .
Gentle and good, she pitied me
And blessed my life with kindness.
Lonely, a cripple, destitute
Still I possessed her love! Ah!
She died! May God be merciful
And let her rest be peaceful.
You're all I have now,
All I have left to comfort me.
Dear God, receive my grateful prayer.

GILDA

Oh, what cruel fate you have endured,
What words could ever express such bit-
    ter woe!
I beg you, Father, say no more!
I cannot bear to see you grieve.
I beg you, tell your name to me,
What sorrow makes you suffer.

RIGOLETTO

Why should I tell you?
Enough of it! Know me as father only.
There may be men who envy me,
And some perhaps who fear me.
Others have placed a curse on me.

GILDA

Patria, parenti, amici,
Voi dunque non avete?

RIGOLETTO

Patri! parenti! amici?
Culto, famiglia, la patria,
Il mio universo è in te!

GILDA

Ah, se può lieto rendervi,
Gioia è la vita a me!
Già da tre lune son qui venuta;
Nè la cittade ho ancor veduta;
Se il concedete, farlo or potrei . . .

RIGOLETTO

Mai! mai! Uscita, dimmi, unqua sei!

GILDA

No.

RIGOLETTO

Guai!

GILDA

(Ah, che dissi?)

RIGOLETTO

Ben te ne guarda!
(Potrian seguirla, rapirla ancora!
Qui d'un buffone si disonora
La figlia, e se ne ride . . . Orror!)
                        (Verso la casa.)
Olà?

(Giovanna esce dalla casa.)

GIOVANNA

Signor?

RIGOLETTO

Venendo mi vede alcuno?
Bada, di il vero . . .

GIOVANNA

Ah no, nessuno.

RIGOLETTO

Sta ben . . . la porta che dà al bastione
È sempre chiusa?

GIOVANNA

Ognor si sta.

RIGOLETTO (a Giovanna.)

Ah, veglia, o donna, questo fiore
Che a te puro confidai;
Veglia attenta, e non sia mai
Che s' offuschi il suo candor.
Tu dei venti dal furore,
Ch' altri fiori hanno piegato,
Lo difendi, e immacolato
Lo ridona al genitor.

GILDA

Quanto affetto! quali cure!
Che temete, padre mio?
Lassù in cielo, presso Dio
Veglia un angiol protettor.
Da noi stoglie le sventure
Di mia madre il priego santo;
Non fia mai disvelto o franto
Questo a voi diletto fiore.
(Il Duca entra in borghese dalla
strada.)

RIGOLETTO

Alcuno v'è fuori . . .
(Apre la porta della corte, a mentre
esce nella strada il Duca guizza furtivo nella corte e si nasconde dietro
l'albero; gettando a Giovanna una
borsa la fa tacere.)

GILDA

Cielo! Sempre novel sospetto.

RIGOLETTO

(a Giovanna tornando.)
Alla chiesa vi seguiva mai nessuno?

GIOVANNA

Mai.

DUCA

(Rigoletto.)

RIGOLETTO

Se talor quí picchian
Guardatevi da aprire.

GIOVANNA

Nemmeno al Duca?

RIGOLETTO

Non che ad altri a lui! Mia figlia,
addio.

DUCA

(Sua figlia!)

GILDA

Addio, mio padre.
(S' abbracciano, e Rigoletto parte chiu-
dendo la porta.)
Giovanna, ho dei rimorsi . . .

GILDA

Have you, O Father, no homeland,
No kin, no friends to cherish?

RIGOLETTO

Homeland and kindred to cherish!
Homeland and kindred, my daughter,
Unite within your person,
You are all I own.

GILDA

To make you happy,
Gladly I'd live for this blessing.
Since we have come here
I've been so lonely,
As my companion Giovanna only.
If you allow me—I might go out . . .

RIGOLETTO
(*suddenly getting excited and worried*)
No, no! Be truthful, have you left the
　house?

GILDA

No!

RIGOLETTO

Don't!

GILDA (*aside*)
Ah, I feel guilty!

RIGOLETTO

Don't ever do it!
If they should find her, they would
　abduct her!
Ah, what delight those villains would
　take
In disgracing me and my daughter!
Hateful thought!

　　　(*calls toward the house*)

Ho, there!

GIOVANNA (*coming from the house*)
My lord!

RIGOLETTO

Did someone observe me coming?
Tell me the truth!

GIOVANNA

Oh no, I'm certain.

RIGOLETTO

That's good . . .
The door to the other entrance is al-
　ways bolted?

GIOVANNA

It always is.

RIGOLETTO (*to Giovanna*)
Ah, guard her always, I implore you
Guard this pure and tender flower,
Guard her well each waking hour,
So that no harm will reach this door.
From the perils of existence
You must shield her with affection;
Keep her safe in your protection
For her father evermore.

GILDA

What affection,
Anxious worry, dearest Father!
Why these cares and apprehensions?
There in heaven, near to God,
A guardian angel prays for me.
My beloved mother's prayer
Will avert all grief and sorrow,
Keep your tender, precious flower
Free from harm for evermore.

RIGOLETTO

Someone is out there . . .

GILDA

Heavens, why is he so suspicious?
(*Rigoletto opens the door of the courtyard, and while he is outside and
looking into the street, the Duke slips
into the courtyard and hides behind
the tree; he throws a purse to Giovanna to make her keep silent.*)

RIGOLETTO
(*re-entering, to Giovanna*)
Are you certain no one followed her
　from church?

GIOVANNA

Yes.

DUKE (*aside, softly*)
Rigoletto!

RIGOLETTO

Never, never open, no matter who may
　come here!

GIOVANNA

With no exception?

RIGOLETTO

There is no exception! Farewell, my
　daughter!

DUKE
His daughter!

GILDA
God speed you.
(*They embrace. Rigoletto leaves, lock-
ing the door behind him.*)
Giovanna, I feel so guilty . . .

GIOVANNA

E perchè mai?

GILDA

Tacqui che un giovin me seguiva al
tempio.

GIOVANNA

Perchè ciò dirgli? l' odiate dunque
Cotesto giovin, voi?

GILDA

No, no, chè troppo è bello e spira
amore.

GIOVANNA

E magnanimo sembra e gran signore.

GILDA

Signor nè principe io lo vorrei;
Sento che povero più l'amerei.
Sognando o vigile sempre lo chiamo,
E l'alma in estasi gli dice: t'a . . .

DUCA

(esce improvviso, fa cenno a Giovanna
d'andarsene, e inginocchiandosi ai
piedi di Gilda termina la frase.)
T'amo!
T'amo; ripetilo sì caro accento;
Un puro schiudimi ciel di contento!

GILDA

Giovanna, Giovanna! Ahi, misera! Non
v'è più alcuno
Che qui rispondami! . . . Oh Dio! . . .
nessuno?

DUCA

Son io coll'anima, che ti rispondo!
Ah, due che s'amano, son tutto un
mondo!

GILDA

Chi mai, chi giungere vi fece a me?

DUCA

S'angelo o demone, che importa a te?
Io t'amo . . .

GILDA

Uscitene.

DUCA

Uscire! Adesso!
Ora che accendene un fuoco istesso!
Ah, inseparabile d'amore il Dio
Stringeva, o vergine, tuo fato al mio!
È il sol dell'anima, la vita è amore,
Sua voce è il palpito del nostro core.
E fama e gloria, potenza e trono,
Umane, fragili qui cose sono,
Una pur avvene sola, divina:
È amor che agl'angeli più ne avvicina!
Adunque amiamoci, donna celeste;
D'invidia agl'uomini sarò per te.

GILDA

Ah, de' miei vergini sogni son queste
Le voci tenere sì care a me!

DUCA

Che m'ami, deh! ripetimi!

GILDA

L'udiste.

DUCA

Oh, me felice!

GILDA

Il nome vostro ditemi . . .
Saperlo non mi lice?

CEPRANO (A Borsa dalla via.)

(Il loco è qui—)

BORSA

(Sta ben—)   (Partono.)

DUCA

Mi nomino . . .   (Pensando.)
Gualtier Maldè
Studente sono e povero.

GIOVANNA (Tornando spaventata.)

Rumor di passi è fuori.

GIOVANNA

But why on earth?

GILDA

One handsome stranger followed me on Sunday.

GIOVANNA

Why should you tell him?
This handsome stranger,
I'm sure you don't dislike him?

GILDA

No, no, his loving glances
Said he adored me . . .

GIOVANNA

He appears to be gen'rous
And very lordly.

GILDA (dreamily)

My lover need not be
A prince or nobleman;
His love means more to me
If in sincerity
He's poor and humble.
Softly and secretly
My heart is calling,
Fervently yearning to say that I love . . .

DUKE

(steps forward suddenly, makes a sign to Giovanna to leave, and, kneeling before Gilda, completes her sentence)

Love you! Say it once more to me
Now we're together!
My love for you will be flaming forever!

GILDA (terrified)

Giovanna, Giovanna!
Oh answer me!
Why have you left me alone,
Deserted here?
Oh heaven, I'm frightened!

DUKE

Beloved, your faith in me shall be requited!
Two loving hearts are their own world united.

GILDA

It is a mystery how you came here!

DUKE

What does it matter now,
What do you fear? I love you!

GILDA

Oh, leave me now!

DUKE

Leave you! What folly!
Now when the ecstasy of love inflames me!
Our guiding stars decree that we are fated
To share one destiny that love created!
Love is the sunlight and spark of creation,
Its power dominates our hearts' pulsation.
Honors and glory and wealth in profusion
Are human weaknesses and vain illusion.
One thing alone there is worth while possessing:
It's love, it's love alone
That gives our lives celestial blessing!
If you belong to me in love united,
That will be paradise,
Heaven on earth,
That will be paradise,
Enjoyed on earth!

GILDA

My secret longing at last came true,
Ah, my hopes and fantasies, the dream of love!

DUKE

You love me—say it once again . . .

GILDA

I love you!

DUKE

How you enchant me!

GILDA

Now may I hear your name at last?
This favor you will grant me?

CEPRANO

(who has approached the house from outside, with Borsa)

The house is here . . .

BORSA

That's right.
(They disappear again.)

DUKE (to Gilda)

Of course you may . . .
(He thinks for a moment.)
Gualtier Maldè—
I am a student—and penniless.

GIOVANNA (enters excitedly)

I hear somebody coming . . .

GILDA
Forse mio padre . . .

DUCA
(Ah cogliere
Potessi il traditore
Che sì mi sturba!)

GILDA (a Giovanna.)
Adducilo
Di quà al bastione . . . or ite . . .

DUCA
Di: m' amerai tu?

GILDA
E voi?

DUCA
L' intera vita . . . poi . . .

GILDA
Non più . . . non più . . . partite.

GILDA, DUCA
Addio, speranza ed anima
Sol tu sarai per me.
Addio, vivrà immutabile
L' affetto mio per te.
(Il Duca entra in casa scortato da Gio-
vanna. Gilda resta fissando la porta
ond' è partito.)

GILDA (sola)
Gualtier Maldè! nome di lui sì amato
Ti scolpisci nel core innamorato!
Caro nome che il mio cor
Festi primo palpitar,
Le delizie dell' amor
Mi dêi sempre rammentar!
Col pensier il mio desir
A te sempre volerà,
E fin l'ultimo sospir,
Caro nome, tuo sarà.
(Sale al terrazzo con una candela.)
(Entrano Marullo, Ceprano, Borsa,
Cortigiani armati e mascherati dalla
via. Gilda sul terrazzo, che tosto entra
in casa.)
BORSA
È là.   (Indicando Gilda al Coro.)

CEPRANO
Miratela.

CORO
Oh, quanto è bella.

MARULLO
Par fata od angiol.

CORO
L'amante è quella
Di Rigoletto!

(Entra Rigoletto concentrato.)

RIGOLETTO
(Riedo! perchè?)

BORSA
Silenzio! all'opra, badate a me.

RIGOLETTO
(Ah, da quel vecchio fui maledetto!)
Chi va là?

BORSA (Ai compagni.)
Tacete . . . c'è Rigoletto.

CEPRANO
Vittoria doppia! L'uccideremo.

BORSA
No, chè domani più rideremo.

MARULLO
Or tutto aggiusto . . .

RIGOLETTO
Chi parla qua?

MARULLO
Ehi! Rigoletto—Di' . . .

RIGOLETTO
                (Con voce terrible.)
Chi va là?

MARULLO
Eh, non mangiarci! Son . . .

RIGOLETTO
Chi?

MARULLO
Marullo.

RIGOLETTO
In tanto buio lo sguardo è nullo.

MARULLO
Quì ne condusse ridevol cosa,
Torre a Ceprano vogliam la sposa.

RIGOLETTO
(Ahimè! respiro!) Ma come entrare?

MARULLO
(a Ceprano) La vostra chiave? (a
Rigoletto) Non dubitare,
Non dee mancarci lo stratagemma,

GILDA (*terrified*)

Maybe my father—

DUKE (*aside*)

The devil take the insolent intruder
Who dares disturb me!

GILDA (*to Giovanna*)

You'd better let him leave by the side
  door,
And hurry . . .

DUKE

You love me, you say?

GILDA

And you?

DUKE

For now and always and . . .

GILDA

No more, no more, I beg you,
My joy and happiness.

BOTH

My heart will always be yours alone!
Farewell, beloved, good-by, my love!
My heart and soul belong to you alone
Forevermore!
(*The Duke leaves quickly, escorted by
  Giovanna.*)

GILDA (*alone*)

Gualtier Maldè! Name of my dear be-
  loved!
Deeply graven in my heart be it forever!
Treasured mem'ry of his name,
Name of him that I adore!
May its bright and glowing flame
Light my soul forevermore!
Ev'ry word he said so dear
I shall keep with tender care
As a precious souvenir
Of the glorious love we share!

BORSA (*softly to the Courtiers*)

She's there.

CEPRANO

How fair she is!

COURTIERS

No beauty rarer!

MARULLO

No queen is fairer!

COURTIERS

She is the mistress of Rigoletto!

RIGOLETTO
(*reappearing, in a state of anxiety*)

Why did I return?

BORSA (*to the Courtiers*)

Attention! Let's hurry,
We must prepare.

RIGOLETTO (*to himself*)

Ah, fateful curse, I cannot forget it!
      (*encountering Borsa, aloud*)
Who goes there?

BORSA (*softly to the Courtiers*)

Be careful, it's Rigoletto!

CEPRANO

So much the better, now we can slay
  him!

BORSA

No, for tomorrow we'll laugh and flay
  him.

MARULLO

It's time for action . . .

RIGOLETTO

Whose voice is that?

MARULLO

Eh! Rigoletto—say—

RIGOLETTO (*in a terrible voice*)

Who goes there?

MARULLO

Why such a fury? I'm—

RIGOLETTO

Who?

MARULLO

Marullo.

RIGOLETTO (*gentler*)

It is so dark here, I could not see you.

MARULLO

We'll fool Ceprano, and when we've
  tricked him
We'll steal his countess, a lovely victim.
    RIGOLETTO (*to himself, relieved*)
I breathe more freely! How will we do
  it?

MARULLO (*softly to Ceprano*)

I need your door key!
          (*to Rigoletto*)
There's nothing to it.
In clever planning none can outwit us.

Ecco la chiave . . .

(*Gli da la chiave.*)

RIGOLETTO (*Palpandola.*)
Sento il suo stemma.
(Ah, terror vano fu dunque il mio!)

(*Respirando.*)
N' è là il palazzo, con voi son io.

MARULLO
Siam mascherati.

RIGOLETTO
Ch' io pur mi mascheri
A me una larva.

MARULLO
Si, pronta è già.
Terrai la scala . . .

(*Gli mette una maschera, e nello stesso
tempo lo benda con un fazzoletto, e
lo pone a reggere una scala, che a-
vranno appostata al terrazzo.*)

RIGOLETTO
Fitta è la tenebra.

MARULLO (*Ai compagni.*)
La benda cieco e sordo il fa.

TUTTI
Zitti, zitti moviamo a vendetta,
Ne sia colto or che men l' aspetta.
Derisore sì audace, costante
A sua volta schernito sarà!
Cheti, cheti, rubiamgli l' amante,
E la corte doman riderà.

(*Alcuni salgono al terrazzo, rompon la
porta del primo piano, scendono,
aprono ad altri ch' entrano dalla
strada, e riescono, trascinando Gilda
la quale avrà la bocca chiusa da un
fazzoletto. Nel traversare la scena ella
perde una sciarpa.*)

GILDA (*Da lontano.*)
Soccorso, padre mio!

CORO
Vittoria!

GILDA (*Più lontano.*)
Aita!

RIGOLETTO
Non han finito ancor! Qual derisione!

(*Si tocca gli occhi.*)
Sono bendato!

(*Si strappa impetuosamente la benda e
la maschera , ed ai chiarore d' una
lanterna scordata riconosce la sciarpa, vede la porta aperta, entra, ne
trae Giovanna spaventata; la fissa
con istupore, si strappa i capelli senza
poter gridare; finalmente dopo molti
sforzi, esclama*)

Ah! la maledizione!

(*Sviene.*)

ATTO III.

*Salotto nel palazzo ducale. Vi sono due
porte laterali, una maggiore nel fondo
ch' è chiusa. Ai suoi lati pendono i
ritratti in tutta figura, a sinistra del
Duca, a destra della sua sposa. V' ha
un seggiolone presso una tavola co-
perta di velluto, ed altri mobili. Il
Duca entra dal mezzo agitato.*

DUCA
Ella mi fu rapita!
E quando o ciel? Ne' brevi istanti,
Prima che il mio presagio interno
Sull' orma corsa ancora mi spingesse!
Schiuso era l' uscio! e la magion de-
serta!
E dove ora sarà quell' angiol caro?
Colei che prima potè in questo core
Destar la fiamma di costanti affetti?
Colei sì pura, al cui modesto sguardo
Quasi spinto a virtù talor mi credo!
Ella mi fu rapita!
E chi l'ardiva? Ma ne avrò vendetta!
Lo chiede il pianto della mia diletta.
Parmi veder le lagrime
Scorrenti da quel ciglio,
Quando fra il dubbio e l'ansia
Del subito periglio,
Dell' amor nostro memore
Il suo Gualtier chiamò.
Ned ei potea soccorrerti,
Cara fanciulla amata;
Ei che vorria coll'anima

(showing Rigoletto the key he has gotten from Ceprano)
His key will admit us.

RIGOLETTO (feeling the key)
Ceprano's emblem!

(to himself)
No need to worry, they bear no malice.

(aloud)
I'll gladly join you, this is his palace.

MARULLO
We all have masks on.

RIGOLETTO
Have you an extra mask
That you will lend me?

MARULLO
Yes, here it is.
You hold the ladder.
(puts a mask on him and at the same time blindfolds him with a handkerchief, and places him holding a ladder against the wall)

RIGOLETTO
How dense the darkness is . . .
MARULLO (softly to the Courtiers)
The blindfold closes his eyes and ears.
(While the following chorus is sung, some Courtiers climb up to the terrace, break open the door of the first story and descend, opening the street entrance to the others.)

COURTIERS
Swiftly moving to finish our mission,
Make no sound to arouse suspicion.
He who always so boldly derides us
Shall for once be the one we will mock.
While he helps us, we steal his beloved
And tomorrow the whole court will laugh.
(Some of the Courtiers have entered the house. They carry Gilda out. While crossing the stage she loses a scarf.)

GILDA (from a distance)
Oh help me, Father, help me!

COURTIERS (from a distance)
Victory!

GILDA
Oh, help me!

RIGOLETTO
(still holding the ladder, blindfolded)
Why does it take so long? It must be over.
(puts his hand to his eyes)
This is a blindfold!
(He violently tears off the mask and the blindfold and, recognizing Gilda's scarf, he sees the broken door, enters the house, drags the stunned Giovanna out. Frantic with despair, he finally cries out:)
Ah—ah—ah—!
The curse of Monterone!

ACT III

Large hall in the ducal palace. There are two side doors, and a large one in the center that closes. At the sides hang the portraits (full-length) of the Duke and his wife. There is a big armchair near a table, covered with a velvet cloth, and other furniture.

DUKE (enters in great agitation)
Treacherous villains stole her!
I came too late! When I had left her,
I had a sudden premonition
She was in danger,
And hastened to protect her.
Futile intention! I found the house deserted!
And where can she be now?
My dear beloved? My lovely angel,
The only one who moved me to real devotion
And constant affection!
She was so pure, her gentle glance so modest,
I became a better man, the more I loved her.
Now she has been abducted!
Who dared to do this?
Let them beware, for I shall take my vengeance!
So I have promised ah, my dear beloved!
Torn from him who adores you,
Despairing, weeping in terror,
Dearest, you must have suffered
Alone in sudden peril.
I seem to hear you calling me,
Your own Gualtier Maldè!
Nowhere I found a trace of you.
Gone was my dear beloved,
Gone all my joy and happiness,

Farti quaggiù beata;
Ei che le sfere agl'angeli
Per te non invidiò.

(*Marullo, Ceprano, Borsa, ed altri
Cortigiani entrano dal mezzo.*)

TUTTI

Duca, duca!

DUCA

Ebben?

TUTTI

L'amante
Fu rapita a Rigoletto.

DUCA

Come? e donde?

TUTTI

Dal suo tetto.

DUCA

Ah. ah! dite, come fu?   (*Siede.*)

TUTTI

Scorrendo uniti remota via,
Brev'ora dopo caduto il dì,
Come previsto ben s'era in pria,
Rara beltà ci si scoprì.
Era l'amante di Rigoletto,
Che vista appena si dileguò.
Già di rapirla s'avea il progetto,
Quando il buffon vêr noi spuntò;
Che di Ceprano noi la contessa
Rapir volessimo, stolto credè;
La scala, quindi, all'uopo messa,
Bendato ei stesso ferma tenè.
Salimmo e rapidi la giovinetta
A noi riusciva quindi asportar.
Quand'ei s'accorse della vendetta
Restò scornato ad imprecar.

DUCA

(Cielo! È dessa! la mia diletta!)

CORO

Ad imprecar,
Restò scornato ad imprecar!

DUCA

Ma dove trovasi la poveretta?

CORO

Fu da noi stessi addotta or qui.

DUCA

(Ah tutto il ciel non mi rapì!)
Possente amor mi chiama,
Volar io deggio a lei;
Il serto mio darei
Per consolar quel cor.
Ah! sappia alfin chi l'ama,
Conosca alfin chi sono,
Apprenda ch'anco in trono
Ha degli schiavi Amor.

CORO

Oh qual pensier or l'agita,
Come cangiò d'umor!

(*Duca esce frettoloso dal mezzo, Rigoletto entra.*)

MARULLO

Povero Rigoletto!

RIGOLETTO

La ra, la ra, la ra, la ra, la ra!

CORO

Ei vien! Silenzio.
Oh buon giorno, Rigoletto.

RIGOLETTO

(Han tutti fatto il colpo!)

CEPRANO

Ch'hai di nuovo, buffon?

RIGOLETTO

Ch'hai di nuovo, buffon?
Che dell'usato
Più noioso voi siete.

CORO

Ah! ah! ah!

RIGOLETTO

La ra, la ra, la ra, la ra, la ra.
(Ove l'avran nascosta?)

TUTTI

(Guardate com' è inquieto!)

RIGOLETTO (*a Marullo.*)

Son felice
Che nulla a voi nuocesse
L' aria di questa notte.

MARULLO

Questa notte!

RIGOLETTO

Sì . . . Oh fu il bel colpo!

Fled in that hour I lost you.
You are my dream of paradise,
You are my world and all.

COURTIERS (*entering animatedly*)
Highness, hear this!

DUKE
What's new?

COURTIERS
We just have snared the mistress of
  Rigoletto!

DUKE
Really? From where?

COURTIERS
From his own house.

DUKE
How you did it, let me hear!

COURTIERS
Last night in secret we all collected
And near Ceprano's house we searched
  around;
In one old mansion, as we expected,
A lovely girl we shortly found.
It was the mistress of Rigoletto,
Whom we beheld there with our own
  eyes,
We had decided to take her with us,
When he came by to our surprise.
And when we told him we were in-
  tending
To steal Ceprano's wife, the fool be-
  lieved;
He held the ladder, not comprehending,
And with a blindfold he was deceived.
And then we rapidly achieved our
  errand,
We seized the girl and carried her away.
When he discovered that he was tricked,
One can imagine his dismay, his great
  dismay!

DUKE (*aside*)
Heavens, they found her, my dear beloved!

COURTIERS
It served him right,
It was a most successful night!

DUKE
Where have you hidden her, poor girl,
  where is she?

COURTIERS
To please your lordship, we brought
  her here.

DUKE
Thank Heaven, she was spared to me!
With all my heart I love her,
I never would betray her.
To lighten her despair
I would throw my crown away.
May she at last discover
The true name of her lover,
That even crown and scepter
Obey the God of love.
(*The Duke rushes off in great haste;
  Rigoletto enters from the center, sim-
  ulating indifference.*)

MARULLO (*with sincere expression*)
Poor Rigoletto!

RIGOLETTO
La ra, la ra, la ra, la ra, la ra!

COURTIERS
(*softly, among themselves*)
He's there, let's watch him.
And how is our Rigoletto?

RIGOLETTO (*to himself*)
They all did this together!

CEPRANO
Any news yet, buffoon?

RIGOLETTO (*imitating Ceprano*)
Any news yet, buffoon?
That you are duller on this morning
  than usual!

COURTIERS
Ha ha ha!

RIGOLETTO
(*moving about on the stage, looking
  around anxiously*)
La ra la ra, la ra, la ra la ra . . .
              (*to himself*)
Where did they hide my darling?

COURTIERS (*among themselves*)
He's searching for his sweetheart!

RIGOLETTO
I am glad that you are not ill this
  morning.
Last night was very chilly.

MARULLO
Very chilly?

RIGOLETTO
Oh, our prank was funny!

MARULLO

S' ho dormito sempre!

RIGOLETTO

Ah, voi dormiste? Avrò dunque sognato!
(*S' allontana, e vedendo un fazzoletto sopra una tavola, ne osserva inquieto la cifra.*)

TUTTI

(Ve' come tutto osserva!)

RIGOLETTO (*Gettandolo.*)

(Non è il suo.)
Dorme il Duca tuttor?

TUTTI

Sì, dorme ancora.
(*Entra un Paggio dalla Duchessa.*)

PAGGIO

Al suo sposo parlar vuol la Duchessa.

CEPRANO

Dorme.

PAGGIO

Qui or or con voi non era?

BORSA

È a caccia.

PAGGIO

Senza paggi! senz' armi!

TUTTI

E non capisci
Che per ora vedere non può alcuno?

RIGOLETTO

(*Che a parte è stato attentissimo al dialogo balzando improvviso tra loro prorompe.*)
Ah ella è qui dunque! Ella è col Duca!

TUTTI

Chi?

RIGOLETTO

La giovin che stanotte
Al mio tetto rapiste—
Ma la saprò riprender! Ella è là!

TUTTI

Se l' amante perdesti, la ricerca altrove.

RIGOLETTO

Io vo' mia figlia!

TUTTI

La sua figlia!

RIGOLETTO

Sì, la mia figlia . . . d'una tal vittoria
Che? . . . Adesso non ridete?
Ella è là! la vogl'io . . . la renderete.

(*Corre verso la porta di mezzo, ma i Cortigiani gli attraversano il passaggio.*)

Cortigiani, vil razza dannata
Per qual prezzo vendeste il mio bene?
A voi nulla per l' oro sconviene,
Ma mia figlia è impagabil tesor.
La rendete . . . o se pur disarmata
Questa man per voi fora cruenta;
Nulla in terra più l' uomo paventa
Se dei figli difende l' onor.
Quella porta, assassini, m' aprite!

(*Si getta ancor sulla porta che gli è nuovamente contesa dai gentiluomini; lotta alquanto, poi torna spossato sul davanti del teatro.*)

Ah! voi tutti a me contro venite!

(*Piange.*)

Ebben piango! Marullo, signore,
Tu ch' hai l' alma gentil come il core
Dimmi tu dove l' hanno nascosta?
È là? Non é vero? tu taci! ohimè!
Miei signori, perdono, pietate
Al vegliardo la figlia ridate
Ridonarla a voi nulla ora costa,
Tutto al mondo è tal figlia per me.

(*Gilda esce dalla stanza a sinistra e si getta nelle paterne braccia.*)

GILDA

Mio padre!

RIGOLETTO

Dio! mia Gilda!

MARULLO (*pretending*)

That I was sleeping soundly?

RIGOLETTO

You were sleeping soundly?
Then I must have been dreaming.
(*He moves away, singing softly, sees a
  handkerchief, and snatches it up.*)
La ra, la ra, la ra, la ra la ra . . .

COURTIERS

Look, look, he picked up a kerchief!

RIGOLETTO (*aside*)

It's not hers.
(*throwing the handkerchief away,
  aloud*)
Is the Duke still asleep?

COURTIERS

Yes, he is sleeping.
(*a page enters*)

PAGE

Will the Duke grant an audience to the
Duchess?

CEPRANO

He's sleeping.

PAGE

That's not true, because I saw him.

BORSA

He went hunting.

PAGE

Unescorted, at this hour?

COURTIERS

Are you so stupid that you don't under-
stand
Why he can't see you?

RIGOLETTO

(*who had stood listening most atten-
tively to the conversation, rushes suddenly toward them*)

Ah, she is in there!
She's in his bedroom!

COURTIERS

Who?

RIGOLETTO (*furiously*)

The girl that you abducted last night
from my dwelling.
But I will be relentless,
Give her back!

COURTIERS

If you're looking for your mistress,
Go and find her elsewhere!
RIGOLETTO (*with terrifying intensity*)
I want my daughter!

COURTIERS (*taken aback*)

Ah, his daughter.

RIGOLETTO

Yes, she's my daughter . . .
Disappointing triumph!
Yes? I see you laugh no longer!
(*rushes toward the door, but the
  Courtiers block his way*)
She is there! Let me see her,
No one shall wrong her!
(*with utmost hatred*)
Fawning courtiers, degraded and lowly,
For what profit have you sold my treas-
ure?
Wanton scoundrels, your gold is your
measure!
But my daughter no ransom could buy!
Give her back now, or I swear by what's
holy,
My revenge shall be bloody and fright-
ful!
There's no power so strong and so
rightful
That a father would not dare defy!
Let me in there, you assassins,
(*Rigoletto struggles with the Courtiers,
  then moves forward, exhausted.*)
Ah, you've banded all together,
Against me, heartless, ev'ry one! (*in
tears*)
Ah, will nothing move you . . .
Marullo, I implore you,
See my tears as I plead here before you.
Tell me where they have hidden my
daughter,
In there? Won't you tell me?
No answer? Woe me!
Noble lords, I implore you, have mercy!
I entreat you, have pity on a father!
Give her back, for to you she means
nothing,
While to me she is dearer
Than all the gold on earth.

GILDA

(*entering from the room at left, throwing herself into her father's arms*)

My father!

RIGOLETTO

Gilda, my Gilda!

Signori, in essa è tutta
La mia famiglia. Non temer più nulla,
Angelo mio, fu scherzo, non è vero?

(*ai cortigiani.*)

Io che pur piansi or rido. (*a Gilda.*)
E tu a che piangi?

GILDA

Ah, l'onta, padre mio.

RIGOLETTO

Cielo! Che dici?

GILDA

Arrossir voglio innanzi a voi soltanto.

RIGOLETTO

(*Rivolto ai Cortigiani con imperioso modo.*)

Ite di quà, voi tutti!
Se il Duca vostro d'appressarsi osasse,
Ch' ei non entri, gli dite, e ch' io ci sono.

(*Si abbandona sul seggiolone.*)

TUTTI (*Tra loro.*)

(Coi fanciulli e co' dementi
Spesso giova il simular.
Partiam pur, ma quel ch' ei tenti
Non lasciamo d' osservar.)

(*Escon dal mezzo e chiudon la porta.*)

RIGOLETTO

Parla, siam soli.

GILDA

(Ciel! dammi coraggio!)

Tutte le feste al tempio
Mentre pregava Iddio,
Bello e fatale un giovane
Offriasi al guardo mio.
Se i labbri nostri tacquero
Dagl'occhi il cor parlò.
Furtivo fra le tenebre
Sol ieri a me giungeva;
Sono studente, povero,
Commosso, mi diceva,
E con ardente palpito
Amor mi protestò.
Partì, partì, il mio core aprivasi
A speme più gradita,

Quando improvvisi apparvero
Color che m'han rapita,
E a forza qui m'addussero
Nell'ansia più crudel.

RIGOLETTO

(Solo per me l' infamia
A te chiedeva, o Dio
Ch' ella potesse ascendere
Quanto caduto er' io.
Ah! presso del patibolo
Bisogna ben l' altare!
Ma tutto ora scompare,
L' altare si rovesciò!)
Piangi, fanciulla, scorrere
Fa il pianto sul mio cor.

GILDA

Padre, in voi parla un angel per me
consolator.

RIGOLETTO

Compiuto pur quanto a fare mi resta
Lasciare potremo quest' aura funesta.

GILDA

Sì.

RIGOLETTO

(E tutto un sol giorno cangiare potè!)
(*Un Usciere, e il Conte di Monterone,
che dalla destra attraversa il fondo
della sala fra gli alabardieri.*)

USCIERE

Schiudete! ire al carcere Monteron
dee.

MONTERONE

(*Fermandosi verso il ritratto.*)

Poichè fosti invano da me maledetto,
Nè un fulmine o un ferro colpiva il tuo
petto,
Felice pur anco, o Duca, vivrai.

(*Esce fra le guardie dal mezzo.*)

RIGOLETTO

No, vecchio, t' inganni
Un vindice avrai.
Sì, vendetta, tremenda vendetta
Di quest' anima è solo desio—
Di punirti già l' ora s' affretta,
Che fatale per te tuonerà.
Come fulmin scagliato da Dio
Te colpire il buffone saprà.

(*to the Courtiers*)
Behold her, my daughter,
My treasure, my one possession!
(*to Gilda*)
Now that I found you,
My darling, fear nothing.
(*to the Courtiers*)
Admit it, you were joking—
Tears are forgotten for laughter . . .
But you, you are trembling?

GILDA

For shame and degradation . . .

RIGOLETTO

Heavens, it can't be!

GILDA

Let no one witness my deep humilia-
tion!

RIGOLETTO

(*turning upon the Courtiers in an im-
perious manner*)
Leave us alone, you traitors,
And if the Duke himself should dare to
return here,
You shall not let him enter,
For I forbid it!

COURTIERS (*among themselves*)

When a man has lost his reason
Better let him have his way.
It is wiser to appease him,
And pretend that we obey.
(*they leave*)

RIGOLETTO

(*turns tenderly to Gilda*)
Tell me . . . they're gone now . . .

GILDA

God, give me courage!
It was in church each Sunday,
While I was humbly praying,
I saw a young man glance at me,
His inner thoughts betraying.
Though our lips were silent,
Yet our eyes began to speak of love.
Yesterday just at eventide,
Suddenly he was near me.
That he was poor he said to me,
And I believed sincerely.
Then with growing ardor
He swore his glowing love.
And then—he left—
So my heart awoke to love
Complete and all prevading.

Suddenly all those men appeared;
By ruthless force invading,
They seized me and abducted me,
And brought me this cruel ordeal.

RIGOLETTO (*to himself*)

Ah, mine be the shame of infamy,
That was my fervent prayer
So that her life be blameless
And heaven protect and spare her.
All men who face eternity
Have one hope for salvation,
But nothing is left me,
No consolation,
My altar is destroyed, ah!
(*turning to Gilda*)
Gilda, Gilda! My daughter!
Let me console you!
I've only one aim now, one goal and
endeavor;
When that is accomplished, we'll leave
here forever!

GILDA

Yes.

RIGOLETTO (*to himself*)

And all this misfortune in one single
day!
(*Count Monterone is led across the
stage between guards.*)

USHER

Make way there,
We are leading Monterone to the
dungeon.

MONTERONE

(*standing still before the portait of the
Duke*)
O Duke,
Since my curse had no power to blight
you,
Since no lightning from heaven de-
scended to smite you,
Live happy forever in pleasure and
vice!
(*He is led away.*)

RIGOLETTO

No, you are mistaken,
An avenger will rise!
Feel the might of my dreadful vendetta!
Sealing your doom is my only desire.
Deeds so evil are wrought by a debtor
Damned by God to the flames and to
ruin.
Though the power that dooms you is
higher,
Fall by the hand of the scornful
buffoon.

GILDA

O mio padre, qual gioia feroce
Balenarvi negli occhi vegg' io!
Perdonate . . . a noi pure una voce
Di perdono dal cielo verrà.
(Mi tradiva, pur l' amo, gran Dio.
Per l' ingrato ti chiedo pietà!
(*Escon del mezzo.*)

ATTO IV.

*Deserta sponda del Mincio. Gilda e
Rigoletto inquieto sono sulla strada.
Sparafucile nell' interno dell' osteria,
seduto presso una tavola, sta ripu-
lendo il suo cinturone, senza nulla
intendere di quanto accade al di
fuori.*

RIGOLETTO

E l' ami?

GILDA

Sempre.

RIGOLETTO

Pure tempo a guarirne t' ho lasciato.

GILDA

Io l'amo.

RIGOLETTO

Povero cor di donna! Ah, il vile infame!
Ma ne avrai vendetta, o Gilda.

GILDA

Pietà, mio padre.

RIGOLETTO

E se tu certa fossi
Ch' ei ti tradisse, l'ameresti ancora?

GILDA

Nol sò, ma pur m' adora.

RIGOLETTO

Egli?

GILDA

Sì.

RIGOLETTO

Ebben, osserva dunque.
(*La conduce presso una delle fessure
del muro, ed ella vi guarda.*)

GILDA

Un uomo vedo.

RIGOLETTO

Per poco attendi.

(*Il Duca, che, in assisa di semplice
officiale di cavalleria entra nella sala
terrena per una porta a sinistra.*)

GILDA

Ah, padre mio!

DUCA (*a Sparafucile.*)

Due cose e tosto!

SPARAFUCILE

Quali?

DUCA

Una stanza e del vino.

RIGOLETTO

(Son questi i suoi costumi!)

SPARAFUCILE

(Oh, il bel zerbino!)
(*Entra nella vicina stanza.*)

DUCA

La donna è mobile
Qual piuma al vento,
Muta d'accento
E di pensiero.
Sempre un amabile
Leggiadro viso,
In pianto o in riso,
È menzognero.
È sempre misero
Chi a lei s'affida,
Chi le confida,
Mal cauto il core!
Pur mai non sentesi
Felice appieno
Chi su quel seno
Non liba amore!

(*Sparafucile rientra con una bottiglia
di vino e due bicchieri, che depone
sulla tavola, quindi batte col pomo
della sua lunga spada due colpi al
soffitto. A quel segnale una ridente
giovane, in costume di zingara scende
a salti la scala. Il Duca corre per
abbracciarla, ma ella gli sfugge.—
Sparafucile uscito sulla via, a parte
a Rigoletto.*)

SPARAFUCILE

E là il vostr' uomo. Viver dee o morire?

RIGOLETTO

Più tardi tornerò l'opra a compire.

(*Gilda e Rigoletto sulla via, il Duca e
Maddalena nel piano terreno.*)

GILDA

Father, Father, although unspoken,
Savage joy fills your heart with longing!
Please forgive him, and by that token
We'll be forgiven by heaven above.
Though he wronged me
I love him in wronging!
God forgive him because of my love!

(*They leave together, in great agitation, through the center door.*)

ACT IV

Near the shore of the river Mincio. It is night. Gilda and Rigoletto are in the street, Sparafucile inside the tavern, sitting by a table, polishing his leather belt, unaware of what is said outside.

RIGOLETTO

You love him?

GILDA

Always.

RIGOLETTO

But I've given you time to forget him.

GILDA

I love him.

RIGOLETTO

Poor tortured heart of woman!
Depraved seducer!
But you'll be avenged, my Gilda.

GILDA

Forgive him, Father.

RIGOLETTO

If I could prove for certain that he betrayed you,
Even then you'd love him?

GILDA

Perhaps . . . but he adores me.

RIGOLETTO

Does he?

GILDA

Yes.

RIGOLETTO

Well then, I'll have to show you.

(*He leads her to one of the chinks in the wall, through which she looks; the Duke, in the uniform of a cavalry officer, enters the tavern.*)

GILDA

I see a man there!

RIGOLETTO

Just wait a little.

GILDA

Ah, Father, spare me!

DUKE (*to Sparafucile*)

Some wine here, and quickly!

SPARAFUCILE

Surely.

DUKE

Go and send me Maddalena!

RIGOLETTO

The game is just beginning.

SPARAFUCILE

A splendid fellow!

(*He goes inside the house.*)

DUKE

Woman's fidelity
Turns like the weather,
Sways like a feather
Tossed in the breezes.
Fond of variety,
She is beguiling,
Frowning or smiling,
Just as she pleases.
Blind in simplicity
Men's hearts are captured,
Wholly enraptured,
Deaf to all warning.
Yet fullest happiness
No man has tasted
Whose life is wasted
Loveless and mourning!

(*Sparafucile reappears with a bottle of wine and two glasses. Then he knocks with the hilt of his long sword against the ceiling. At this signal a young girl enters. She wears gypsy attire. The Duke wants to embrace her, but she escapes him. Meanwhile Sparafucile has gone out on the street and talks to Rigoletto, who reappears at the outside of the tavern.*)

SPARAFUCILE

(*coming into the street*)

I have your man here.
Give your orders, I obey you.

RIGOLETTO

Detain him for a while and then I'll pay you.

(*Gilda and Rigoletto are outside the house, Maddalena and the Duke inside, on the ground floor.*)

DUCA

Un dì, se ben rammentomi,
O bella, t'incontrai!
Mi piacque di te chiedere
E intesi che qui stai.
Or sappi che d'allora
Sol te quest'alma adora.

GILDA

Iniquo!

MADDALENA

Ah! ah! e vent'altre appresso
Le scorda forse adesso?
Ha un'aria il signorino
Da vero libertino . . .

DUCA

Sì, un mostro son . . .

GILDA

Ah, padre mio!

MADDALENA

Lasciatemi, stordito.

DUCA

Ih, che fracasso!

MADDALENA

Stia saggio.

DUCA

E tu sii docile,
Non farmi tanto chiasso.
Ogni saggezza chiudesi
Nel gaudio e nell' amore.

(*Le prende la mano.*)

La bella mano candida!

MADDALENA

Scherzate voi, signore.

DUCA

No, no.

MADDALENA

Son brutta.

DUCA

Abbracciami.

GILDA

Iniquo!

MADDALENA

Ebro!

DUCA

D'amor ardente.

MADDALENA

Signor l' indifferente,
Vi piace canzonar?

DUCA

No, no, ti vo' sposar.

MADDALENA

Ne voglio la parola.

DUCA (*Ironico.*)

Amabile figliuola!

RIGOLETTO (*a Gilda.*)

E non ti basta ancor?

GILDA

Iniquo traditor!

DUCA

Bella figlia dell' amore,
Schiavo son de' vezzi tuoi;
Con un detto sol tu puoi
Le mie pene consolar.
Vieni, e senti del mio core
Il frequente palpitar.

GILDA

Ah, così parlar d' amore!
A me pur l' infame ho udito
Infelice cor tradito,
Per angoscia non scoppiar.

MADDALENA

Ah! ah! rido ben di core,
Chè tal baie costan poco;
Quanto valga il vostro giuoco,
Mel credete, so apprezzar.
Sono avvezza, bel signore,
Ad un simile scherzar.

RIGOLETTO

Taci, il piangere non vale;
Ch' ei mentiva, sei sicura.
Taci, e mia sarà la cura
La vendetta d' affrettar.
Pronta fia, sarà fatale;
Io saprollo fulminar.

M' odi, ritorna a casa,
Oro prendi, un destriero,
Una veste viril che t' apprestai,
E per Verona parti.
Sarovvi io pur doman.

DUKE

One day I saw you smile at me,
I looked at you enraptured.
Your beauty so excited me
My heart was bound and captured.
As no one else before you
Sincerely I adore you.

GILDA

The traitor!

MADDALENA

Ha ha! No one else before me!
You're telling me a story.
A libertine, believe me,
Could never once deceive me.

DUKE

Yes, I'm very bad . . .

GILDA

Ah, dearest father!

MADDALENA

Enough of that, it's silly.

DUKE

Come, don't be naughty!

MADDALENA

Be good now.

DUKE

Don't act so prudishly,
Why suddenly be haughty?
Cast all your foolish qualms away.
My darling, you must surrender.
            (takes her hand)
Your hand is white as ivory!

MADDALENA

You're mocking me, pretender!

DUKE

No, no!

MADDALENA

I'm ugly.

DUKE

I long for you—

GILDA

Betrayer!

MADDALENA

Liar!

DUKE

—with glowing passion!

MADDALENA

It seems to be your fashion
To jest your way through life!

DUKE

I want you for my wife!

MADDALENA

Your promise binds forever!

DUKE

You're lovable and clever!

RIGOLETTO (to Gilda)

You want to hear still more?

GILDA

My heart can bear no more!

DUKE

Maddalena I adore you
You enslave me and enchant me;
Only this one favor you must grant me
Come and love me, be my radiant guid-
        ing star.
I implore you, don't refuse me
Be my radiant guiding star!

GILDA

I believed him, now he betrays me!
Ah, it breaks my heart!
All my trust and my devotion
He has scorned and now I am betrayed,
For all my love and my devotion,
He repaid me with deception.
How I loved him and adored him
And by him I am betrayed, ah—
And he, he broke my heart.

MADDALENA

Talk is cheap, there's no denying
But your compliments amuse me;
Pretty speeches don't confuse me
I know well how false they are.
Many times I heard that story,
To believe it would be madness,
Ha ha ha ha! Ridiculous!

RIGOLETTO

Quiet, your crying now is useless!
He was lying, I have proved it,
But I give you my assurance
That his crime shall be avenged.
All my power and endurance
I'll employ on grim revenge,
I am prepared to strike a fatal blow.

Listen: you must go home now.
Take some money, then on horseback
You will travel,
Disguised as a man, to Verona;
Tomorrow I will join you.

GILDA

Or venite . . .

RIGOLETTO

Impossibil.

GILDA

Tremo.

RIGOLETTO

Va.   (*Gilda parte.*)

(*Sparafucile esce della casa e s'incontra
    come d'accordo con Rigoletto.*)

RIGOLETTO

Venti scudi hai tu detto? Eccone dieci,
E dopo l'opra il resto.
Ei qui rimane?

SPARAFUCILE

Sì.

RIGOLETTO

Alla mezzanotte ritornerò.

SPARAFUCILE

Non cale.
A gettarlo nel fiume basto io solo.

RIGOLETTO

No, no, il vo' far io stesso.

SPARAFUCILE

Sia! Il suo nome?

RIGOLETTO

Vuoi saper anche il mio?
Egli è *Delitto, Punizion* son io.

    (*Parte. Il cielo si oscura e tuona.*)

SPARAFUCILE

La tempesta è vicina!
Più scura fia la notte.

DUCA (*Per prenderla.*)

Maddalena!

MADDALENA

Aspettate . . . mio fratello viene.

DUCA

Che importa?   (*S'ode il tuono.*)

MADDALENA

Tuona!

SPARAFUCILE (*Entrando.*)

E pioverà fra poco.

DUCA

Tanto meglio. Tu dormirai
In scuderia, all' inferno, ove vorrai.

SPARAFUCILE

Oh, grazie.

MADDALENA (*Piano al Duca.*)

Ah, no, partite.

DUCA

Con tal tempo?

SPARAFUCILE

(*Piano a Maddalena.*)

(Son venti scudi d'oro.)
                    (*Al Duca.*)

Ben felice d' offrirvi una stanza. Se a
    voi piace tosto a vederla andiamo.

(*Prende un lume e s' avvia per la
    scala.*)

DUCA

Ebben, sono con te . . . presto, vediamo.

(*Dice una parola all' orecchio de Mad-
    dalena e segue Sparafucile.*)

MADDALENA

Povero giovin! grazioso tanto! (*Tuona.*)
Dio! qual notte è questa!

DUCA

(*Giunto al granaio, vedendone il bal-
    cone senza imposte.*)

Si dorme all' aria aperta? bene, bene!
Buona notte.

SPARAFUCILE

Signor, vi guardi Iddio.

DUCA

Breve sonno dormiam; stanco son io.
La donna è mobile,
Qual piuma al vento,
Muta d'accento,
E di pensiero.
La donna è mobil,
Muta d'accento,
E di pensier,
Muta d'accento e di pen . . .

GILDA

Please come with me!

RIGOLETTO

Impossible!

GILDA

I'm frightened!

RIGOLETTO

Go.

(*Gilda leaves. Rigoletto is joined by Sparafucile, receiving some money from him.*)

RIGOLETTO

We agreed on twenty scudi? Here you have ten.
The rest when it is over.
Will he remain here?

SPARAFUCILE

Yes.

RIGOLETTO

On the stroke of midnight I shall return.

SPARAFUCILE

Don't bother.
I don't need you to throw him in the river.

RIGOLETTO

No, no, I myself must do that.

SPARAFUCILE

All right then. What's his name?

RIGOLETTO

Shall I tell you mine also?
His name is "Guilt," mine is "Just retribution."
(*He leaves. A flash of lightning is seen.*)

SPARAFUCILE (*to himself*)

Soon a storm will be raging,
And there will be no moonlight.

DUKE (*is about to embrace her*)

Maddelena . . .

MADDALENA

Wait till later,
My brother is returning.
(*frequent lightning and thunder, the storm is increasing in force*)

DUKE

Why should I?

MADDALENA

It's thund'ring.

SPARAFUCILE (*entering*)

And soon it will be raining.

DUKE

Even better! Now you can go,
Sleep where you want to,
For all I care, go to the devil.

SPARAFUCILE (*good-humored*)

I thank you!

MADDALENA (*softly to the Duke*)

No, you must leave.

DUKE

In this weather?

SPARAFUCILE (*aside to Maddalena*)

He'll earn us twenty scudos.
(*aloud to the Duke*)
I'll be happy to offer you my own room,
If you allow me, I will let you see it.

DUKE

Well then, I'll go with you,
Quickly, so be it.
(*He whispers something to Maddalena, then follows Sparafucile to the upper story.*)

MADDALENA

Poor trusting stranger! He is so handsome.
(*lightning and thunder*)
Heavens, the storm is frightful!

DUKE (*in the attic*)

This is the peak of luxury!
Really charming! I will stay here.

SPARAFUCILE

Good night, may God protect you!
(*He descends to the ground floor.*)

DUKE

I shall sleep for a while,
I'm feeling tired.
(*He stretches out on the bed, and while singing, he gradually falls asleep.*)
Woman's fidelity
Turns like the weather,
Sways like a feather,
Tossed in the breezes . . .
Beguiling . . . capricious . . .
Sways like a feather,
Never the same,
She'll never be the . . .
(*He is asleep.*)

MADDALENA

È amabile invero cotal giovinotto.

SPARAFUCILE

Oh sì, venti scudi ne dà di prodotto . . .

MADDALENA

Sol venti? son pochi! valeva di più.

SPARAFUCILE

La spada, s'ei dorme, va, portami giù.
(*Gilda comparisce nel fondo della via
in costume virile, con stivali, e spe-
roni.*)

GILDA

A più non ragiono!
Amor mi trascina! Mio padre, perdono!
(*Tuona.*)
Qual notte d' orrore!
Gran Dio, che accadrà?

MADDALENA

Fratello!
(*Sarà discesa ed avrà posata la spada
del Duca sulla tavola.*)

GILDA

Chi parla?

SPARAFUCILE

(*Frugando in un credenzone.*)
Al diavol ten va.

MADDALENA

Somiglia un Apollo quel giovine . . . io
l'amo
Ei m'ama, riposi, nè più l'uccidiamo.

GILDA

O cielo!

SPARAFUCILE

Rattoppa quel sacco!

MADDALENA

Perchè?

SPARAFUCILE

Entr'esso il tuo Apollo, sgozzato da me,
Gettar dovrò al fiume.

GILDA

L'inferno qui vedo!

MADDALENA

Eppure il danaro salvarti scommetto,
Serbandolo in vita.

SPARAFUCILE

Difficile il credo.

MADDALENA

M'ascolta: anzi facil ti svelo un pro-
getto.
De' scudi già dieci dal gobbo ne avesti;
Venire cogli altri più tardi il vedrai—
Uccidilo, e venti allora ne avrai,
Così tutto il prezzo goder si potrà.

GILDA

Che sento! mio padre!

SPARAFUCILE

Uccider quel gobbo! che diavol dicesti!
Un ladro son forse? Son forse un
bandito?
Qual altro cliente da me fu tradito?
Mi paga quest' uomo, fedele m' avrà.

MADDALENA

Ah grazia per esso!

SPARAFUCILE

E duopo ch'ei muoia.

MADDALENA (*Va per salire.*)
Fuggire il fo adesso!

GILDA

Oh buona figliuola!

SPARAFUCILE (*Trattenendola.*)
Gli scudi perdiamo.

MADDALENA

È ver!

SPARAFUCILE

Lascia fare.

MADDALENA

Salvarlo dobbiamo.

SPARAFUCILE

Se pria ch' abbia il mezzo la notte
toccato
Alcuno qui giunga, per esso morrà.

MADDALENA

E' buia la notte, il ciel troppo irato,
Nessuno a quest' ora da qui passerà.

MADDALENA (*in the room below*)
I like that young stranger,
He's handsome and gentle.

SPARAFUCILE
For twenty gold scudos I'm not sentimental.

MADDALENA
Just twenty? That's nothing! A very low fee.

SPARAFUCILE
My dagger, go get it. Go, bring it to me.

GILDA
(*appearing outside, in man's clothes, with boots and spurs*)
I reason no longer,
My heart is commanding, forgive me, dear father!
(*thunder*)
Oh night filled with horror!
And how will it end?

MADDALENA
My brother—
(*She brings the dagger to Sparafucile.*)

GILDA
Who spoke there?

SPARAFUCILE
(*He rummages in a drawer of the cupboard.*)
The devil with you!

MADDALENA
Not even Adonis is handsomer,
I love him, he loves me,
For my sake, O Brother, don't kill him!

GILDA
Good heavens!

SPARAFUCILE
This sack must be mended.

MADDALENA
And why?

SPARAFUCILE
To cover your friend in his watery grave,
Below in the river.

GILDA
Unholy betrayers!

MADDALENA
Suppose we could spare him without any danger,
And still get your money?

SPARAFUCILE
And how would you do that?

MADDALENA
Just listen:
I'll explain how to do it, my brother:
One half of your fee you have gotten already;
At midnight the hunchback will bring you the other.
Let him die as victim instead of the stranger
This way all the money is ours just the same.

GILDA
Great heavens, my father!

SPARAFUCILE
To murder the hunchback? What are you suggesting!
For what do you take me? A thief or a robber?
Since when have I every betrayed any client?
He pays for my service, I'll stand by my word.

MADDALENA
I beg you to spare him!

SPARAFUCILE
No, no, I must kill him!

MADDALENA (*wants to go upstairs*)
I'm going to warn him!

GILDA
Thank God for her pity!

SPARAFUCILE (*holding her back*)
We're losing the money.

MADDALENA
I know!

SPARAFUCILE
I must kill him!

MADDALENA
I beg you to spare him!

SPARAFUCILE
If someone should come here ere midnight has sounded
Let him be the victim, your man may go free.

MADDALENA
The night is too stormy, that hope is unfounded,
So late in such weather what chance could there be?

GILDA

Oh, qual tentazione!
Morir per l'ingrato!
Morire! E mio padre!
O cielo, pietà!

(*Battono le undici e mezzo.*)

SPARAFUCILE

Ancor c'è mezz'ora.

MADDALENA

Attendi fratello . . .

GILDA

Che! Piange tal donna!
Nè a lui darò aita!
Ah, s'egli al mio amore divenne rubello,
Io vo' per la sua gettar la mia vita.

(*Picchia alla porta.*)

MADDALENA

Si picchia?

SPARAFUCILE

Fu il vento.

MADDALENA

Si picchia, ti dico.

SPARAFUCILE

È strano! Chi è!

GILDA

Pietà d'un mendico;
Asil per la notte a lui concedete.

MADDALENA

Fia lunga tal notte!

SPARAFUCILE

Alquanto attendete.

(*Va a cercare nel credenzone.*)

MADDALENA

Su spicciati, presto, fa l'opra compita:
Anelo una vita con altra salvar.

SPARAFUCILE

Ebbene, son pronto; quell'uscio di-
schiudi;
Più ch'altro gli scudi, mi preme salvar.

GILDA

Ah! presso alla morte, sì giovane sono!
Oh ciel, per quegl'empi ti chieggo per-
dono!
Perdona tu, o padre, a quest'infelice!
Sia l'uomo felice ch'or vado a salvar.

MADDALENA

Spicciati!

SPARAFUCILE

Apri!

MADDALENA

Entrate!

GILDA

Dio! loro perdonate!

MADDALENA, SPARAFUCILE

Entrate!

(*Sparafucile amazza e trascina via
Gilda.*)

(*Rigoletto solo si avanza da fondo della
scena chiuso nel suo mantello.*)

RIGOLETTO

Della vendetta alfin giunge l' instante!
Da trenta dì l'aspetto
Di vivo sangue a lagrime piangendo
Sotto la larva del buffon. Quest uscio!

(*Esaminando la casa.*)

È chiuso! Ah, non è tempo ancor!
S'attenda.
Qual notte di mistero!
Una tempesta in cielo!
In terra un omicidio!
Oh come invero quì grande mi sento!

(*Suona mezzanotte.*)

Mezzanotte!

SPARAFUCILE

Chi è là?

RIGOLETTO

Son io.

SPARAFUCILE

Sostate.

(*Rientra e torna trascinando un sacco.*)

È quà spento il vostr' uomo.

RIGOLETTO

Oh gioia! Un lume!

SPARAFUCILE

Un lume? No, il danaro!
Lesti, all' onda il gettiam.

RIGOLETTO (*Gli da una borsa.*)

No, basto io solo.

GILDA

There's one way to save him,
May God give me courage!
Oh heaven forgive me,
Have mercy on me!

(*A clock strikes.*)

SPARAFUCILE

One half hour more . . .

MADDALENA

Be patient my brother—

GILDA

Ah, she's trying to save him
And I do not help her!
Although he has broken
The vow he has sworn me,
I'm willing to die
If his life can be spared.

(*She knocks at the door.*)

MADDALENA

Who's knocking?

SPARAFUCILE

The wind . . .

MADDALENA

I'm sure someone's knocking.

SPARAFUCILE

That's strange! Who's there?

GILDA (*from outside*)

A poor homeless beggar;
I'm asking for shelter for the night only.

MADDALENA

We'll give him his shelter!

SPARAFUCILE

In just a few moments.

(*He goes to the cupboard.*)

MADDALENA

You gave me your promise,
Why wait any longer?
The life of this beggar
Is all that you need!

SPARAFUCILE

So be it, I'm ready.
His life won't concern me,
As long as he'll earn me
    the gold for the deed.

GILDA

As death lies before me,
I pray for the living.
Oh God save these sinners,
Be kind and forgiving.
Forgive me, my father,
That I must leave you;
My life I am giving
So he may live.

MADDALENA

Hurry!

SPARAFUCILE

Open!

MADDALENA

Be welcome!

GILDA (*entering*)

God, grant them your pardon!

MADDALENA, SPARAFUCILE

Be welcome!

(*Sparafucile posts himself behind the door with his dagger. Maddalena opens the door, Sparafucile stabs Gilda.*)

RIGOLETTO

(*returns, wrapped in a cloak*)

This is the moment,
The supreme hour of vengeance!
Full thirty days I've waited,
With searing anguish and tears of desperation,
Under the jester's grinning mask.

(*He goes to Sparafucile's house.*)

The entrance is bolted.
The time has not yet come. I'll wait here.
Oh night of looming myst'ry!
Tempests arise in heaven
And here on earth a murder.
Oh how I savor the rapture of greatness!

(*It sounds midnight.*)

It is midnight.

(*He knocks at the door.*)

SPARAFUCILE

Who's there?

RIGOLETTO

Your client.

SPARAFUCILE

One moment.

(*He goes back and returns, dragging a sack out.*)

Here's the body of your victim.

RIGOLETTO (*joyfully*)

Let's see him! A lantern!

SPARAFUCILE (*hastily*)

A lantern? No. The money!
Hurry, let's throw him in the river.

RIGOLETTO (*gives him a purse*)

No, I don't need you.

SPARAFUCILE

Come vi piace. Qui men atto è il sito.
Più avanti è più profondo il gorgo.
Presto,
Che alcun non·vi sorprenda.
Buona notte.   (*Esce.*)

RIGOLETTO

Egli è là! Morto!
Oh sì!
Vorrei vederlo!
Ma che importa?
È ben desso! Ecco i suoi sproni.
Ora mi guarda, o mondo!
Quest'è un buffone,
Ed un potente è questo!
Ei sta sotto i miei piedi!
È desso! Oh gioia!
È giunta alfine la tua vendetta, o
      duolo!
Sia l'onda a lui sepolcro,
Un sacco il suo lenzuolo!
All'onda! all'onda!

(*Fa per trascinare il sacco verso la
sponda, quando è sorpreso dalla lon-
tana voce del Duca che nel fondo
attraversa la scena.*)

Qual voce! illusion notturna è questa!
No! no! Egli è desso!
Maledizione! Olà, dimon bandito!
                        (*Verso la casa.*)
Chi è mai, chi è qui in sua vece?
                        (*Taglia il sacco.*)
Io tremo. È umano corpo!
                        (*Lampeggia.*)
Mia figlia! Dio! mia figlia!
Ah, no! è impossibil!
Per Verona è in via!
Fu vision! . . . È dessa!
Oh mia Gilda! fanciulla, a me rispondi!
L'assassino mi svela.
Olà! Nessuno? Nessun!
Mia figlia! Mia Gilda! Oh, mia figlia!

GILDA

Chi mi chiama?

RIGOLETTO

Ella parla! . . . Si muove!
È viva! . . . Oh Dio!
Ah, mio ben solo in terra
Mi guarda, mi conosci.

GILDA

Ah, padre mio!

RIGOLETTO

Qual mistero! che fu? dimmi, sei tu
      ferita?

GILDA

L'acciar qui mi piagò . . .

RIGOLETTO

Chi t'ha colpita?

GILDA

V' ho ingannato. Colpevole fui.
L' amai troppo. Ora muoio per lui.

RIGOLETTO

(Dio tremendo! Ella stessa fu colta
Dallo stral di mia giusta vendetta!)
Angiol caro, mi guarda, m'ascolta!
Parla, parlami, figlia diletta!

GILDA

Ah, ch' io taccia! A me, a lui per-
      donate.
Benedite alla figlia, o mio padre.
Lassù in cielo, vicina alla madre,
In eterno per voi pregherò.

RIGOLETTO

Non morir, mio tesoro, pietade.
Mia colomba, lasciarmi non dei,
No, lasciarmi non dei.

GILDA

Lassù in cielo, vicina alla madre,
In eterno per voi pregherò.

RIGOLETTO

No, lasciarmi non dei, non morir.
Se t'involi, qui sol rimarrei.
Non morire, o qui teco morrò!

GILDA

Non più! A lui perdonate.
Mio padre, addio!

RIGOLETTO

Gilda! Mia Gilda! È morta!
Ah, la maledizione!
(*Strappandosi i capelli cade sul cada-
vere della figlia.*)

FINE

SPARAFUCILE

Do as you please.
Here the water is shallow,
But further on, it gets deeper.
Hurry, be careful no one sees you.
Pleasant journey.

(*He re-enters the house.*)

RIGOLETTO (*gloating*)

There he is! Lifeless, at last!
I'd like to see him!
But why should I?
I am certain! I feel his spurs here!
Now let the world observe me!
Here stands a jester,
There lies a mighty ruler!
See me stamp on my master!
No other! In glory!
I have avenged you,
My dear beloved daughter!
A sack will be his coffin,
His graveyard the flowing water!
The water! The water!

(*He is about to drag the sack to the
river, when he hears the voice of the
Duke, who crosses the stage in the
rear while disappearing in the distance.*)

That voice!
It's a dream, a foolish nightmare!
No, it's his voice!

(*He shouts toward the house.*)

Hell and damnation!
Ho there, you fiend, you demon!
Then who can be my victim?
I tremble . . . A human being . . .

(*He cuts the sack, lightning illumi-
nates the scene.*)

My daughter, God, my daughter!
Ah no, it can't be!
She has gone to Verona!
Do I dream?

(*more lightning*)

My Gilda! Oh my Gilda!
My darling, speak to your father!
Tell me how this has happened!
Ho there! No answer! They're gone!
My daughter? My Gilda? Oh my
daughter!

GILDA

(*in a weak voice*)

Who is calling?

RIGOLETTO

She is speaking! She hears me!
She sees me! Oh God, ah—
Beloved, my treasure,
My darling—say you know me . . .

GILDA

Ah, my dear father!

RIGOLETTO

Tragic myst'ry! Oh God!
How did it happen? Tell me . . .

GILDA

The dagger . . . here . . . here through
my heart . . .

RIGOLETTO (*in desperation*)

Who dared to strike you?

GILDA (*with effort, feebly*)

Alone I am guilty . . .
I deceived you.
I adored him . . . Now I die for my
lover!

RIGOLETTO

God Almighty, my own innocent
daughter
Bore the wrath and the force of my
vengeance!
I implore you to hear me, my
daughter
Only speak to me, speak to your father!

GILDA

Ah, do not ask me! Forgive me!
Give your blessing to your daughter, oh
my father . . .
Soon I will be with my mother in
heaven.
There near God I'll be praying for you.

RIGOLETTO

Do not die, I implore you, don't leave
me,
My only child, do not leave me alone,
All alone here on earth!

GILDA

Soon I will be with my mother in
heaven,
There near God I'll be praying for you.

RIGOLETTO

Without you I have no one left on this
earth.
Do not die, I implore you, my child!

GILDA

No more . . . forgive him . . .
My father . . . I'll pray for . .

RIGOLETTO

Gilda! My Gilda! My daughter!

(*He throws himself upon the body of
his daughter in utter despair.*)

Ah! The curse of Monterone!

END OF THE OPERA